Statues and Monuments

JILL FORAN

WEIGL PUBLISHERS INC.

Project Coordinator
Tina Schwartzenberger

Design
Janine Vangool

Layout
Bryan Pezzi

Substantive Editor
Heather C. Hudak

Copy Editor
Jennifer Nault

Photo Researcher
Wendy Cosh

Published by Weigl Publishers Inc.
350 5th Avenue, Suite 3304
New York, NY USA 10118-0069
Web site: www.weigl.com

Library of Congress Cataloging-in-Publication Data

Foran, Jill.
  Statues and monuments / Jill Foran.
     v. cm. -- (American symbols)
Includes bibliographical references and index.
Contents: The Statue of Liberty -- The Washington Monument -- The Lincoln Memorial -- Mount Rushmore -- National memorials -- Map of national statues and monuments -- Chart of national statues and monuments.
  ISBN 1-59036-131-8 (library bound : alk. paper)
  1. National monuments--United States--Juvenile literature. 2. Statues--United States--Juvenile literature. 3. United States--History, Local--Juvenile literature. [1. National monuments. 2. Statues. 3. United States--History, Local.] I. Title. II. Series.
  E159.F685 2004
  973--dc21
                            2003005032

Printed in the United States of America
1 2 3 4 5 6 7 8 9 0   07 06 05 04 03

Photograph Credits
Every reasonable effort has been made to trace ownership and to obtain permission to reprint copyright material. The publishers would be pleased to have any errors or omissions brought to their attention so that they may be corrected in subsequent printings.

Cover: Statue of Liberty (Getty Images, Inc.); **COMSTOCK, Inc.:** page 6/7; **CORBIS/MAGMA:** page 17M (Wolfgang Kaehler); **Getty Images, Inc.:** pages 1, 4, 8/9, 12/13, 14B, 17T, 22; **Bruce Leighty:** page 13B; **National Park Service:** pages 3, 9B, 16M, 16B, 17B; **Bryan Pezzi:** page 23; **PhotoSpin, Inc.:** pages 5R, 7B, 15T; **Keith Stanley:** pages 10/11, 14M, 15B; **Jim Steinhart of www.PlanetWare.com:** pages 5L, 11T, 15M, 16T; **US Army Photo:** page 14T.

Contents

Introduction

The United States has a long and exciting history. Across the country, American citizens create special memorials to pay tribute to this history. A memorial is something that honors the memory of a person or an event. Memorials come in many forms. They can be buildings or parks. They can also be paintings or poems. Memorials can even be special songs. Some of the best-known memorials are statues and monuments.

In 1956, Bedloe's Island in New York was renamed Liberty Island. The Statue of Liberty is located on this island.

Many of the United States's statues and monuments are important national symbols. This means that they represent something about America. Statues and monuments stand for freedom and **justice**. They also remind U.S. citizens of their country's achievements. The Statue of Liberty, the Washington Monument, the Lincoln Memorial, and Mount Rushmore are among the most recognized statues and monuments in the United States.

More than 1,000 men died on the *USS Arizona* when Pearl Harbor was attacked. The memorial honors these men and other military personnel who were killed in the Pacific during World War II.

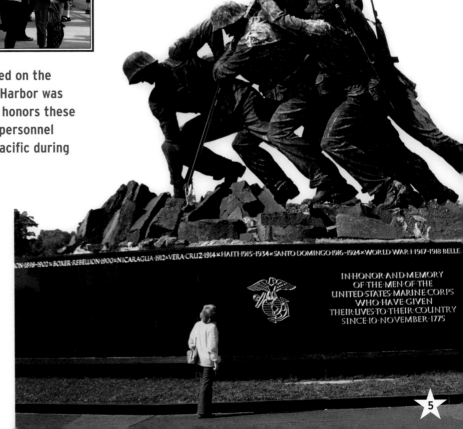

Ten panels at the base of the Iwo Jima Memorial provide information about the battle on the Japanese island of Iwo Jima.

The Statue of Liberty

The Statue of Liberty is a symbol of freedom. It stands on Liberty Island in New York City. The statue was a gift from the people of France. The statue honors the alliance, or friendship, between France and the United States during the **American Revolution**. The Statue of Liberty was completed in France in 1884. It was taken apart and shipped to the United States by boat. When the statue arrived at New York Harbor, it was placed on a very large **pedestal**. In 1886, the Statue of Liberty was dedicated to the soldiers who fought for America's **independence** from Great Britain.

The Statue of Liberty is located near Ellis Island. For many years, this island was an entrance to the United States. From 1892 to 1954, millions of **immigrants** sailed past the Statue of Liberty on their way to Ellis Island. The statue represented their freedom in a new land. The Statue of Liberty shows a woman escaping from the chains of **tyranny**. She wears a crown with seven spikes. These spikes represent the seven seas and seven continents. She holds a torch in her right hand and a **tablet** in her left hand. The torch is a symbol of liberty, or freedom. Written on the tablet is the date July 4, 1776. This was the day the United States announced its independence from Great Britain.

Twenty-five windows fill the Statue of Liberty's crown.

DID YOU KNOW?

★ The true name of the Statue of Liberty is *Liberty Enlightening the World*.

★ From torch to feet, the Statue of Liberty stands 151 feet tall.

★ Visitors to the Statue of Liberty can climb 354 steps to reach the crown.

★ The Statue of Liberty weighs 225 tons.

★ In 1903, poet Emma Lazarus wrote a poem about the Statue of Liberty. It is called *The New Colossus*. The poem appears at the base of the statue.

Washington Monument

The Washington Monument is located in Washington, D.C. It is a memorial to George Washington, the first president of the United States. Washington was a powerful leader. He served as the president from 1789 to 1797. He also led U.S. forces during the American Revolution. Washington is known as "The Father of Our Country." He was given this name for helping to create the United States.

George Washington died in 1799. Many Americans mourned his death. They wanted to honor his memory with a special monument. In 1833, the Washington National Monument Society was formed. This group began to raise money to build a memorial for Washington. In 1847, construction began on the memorial.

The **cornerstone** for the Washington Monument was laid on July 4, 1848. About forty years later, the monument was finally opened to the public. Today, people from all over the world visit the Washington Monument. There are 188 carved stones inside the monument. The stones came from individuals, groups, cities, states, and other countries.

The Washington Monument stands 555 feet tall. It is one of the tallest stone structures in the world.

DID YOU KNOW?

★ Fifty flags surround the base of the Washington Monument. The flags represent the fifty states of the **Union**.

★ The Washington Monument is built in the shape of an Egyptian **obelisk**. On the top is a small pyramid made of solid aluminum.

★ The walls of the Washington Monument are made of marble that came from Maryland and Massachusetts.

★ There is an observation room near the top of the Washington Monument. Visitors can reach this room by climbing 897 steps or by taking an elevator.

WASHINGTON MONUMENT

The Lincoln Memorial

The Lincoln Memorial is also located in Washington, D.C. This national memorial honors Abraham Lincoln, the sixteenth president of the United States. He governed the U.S. between 1861 and 1865, the time of the **Civil War**. Lincoln fought to keep the United States together. He also worked to ensure that all people living in the United States had equal rights and freedoms. After Abraham Lincoln was **assassinated**, U.S. citizens built a memorial to him. In 1901, a site at West Potomac Park was chosen for the memorial. Construction began on February 12, 1914. Carvers, designers, and painters worked on the memorial for 8 years.

From the outside, the Lincoln Memorial looks like a Greek **temple**. It has thirty-six columns, or pillars. The columns represent the number of states in the Union when Lincoln died. A large statue of Abraham Lincoln sits between the columns. The statue is a reminder of the importance of freedom and unity.

Many historic events have taken place at the Lincoln Memorial.

★ The statue of Abraham Lincoln is 19 feet tall and weighs 175 tons. Twenty-eight blocks of white marble that came from Georgia were used to make the statue.

★ There are two murals, or large wall paintings, inside the Lincoln Memorial. These murals show important events that took place during Lincoln's presidency.

★ Beneath each mural in the Lincoln Memorial is a stone tablet. Each tablet shows speeches made by Lincoln.

★ When the Lincoln Memorial was completed in 1922, there were forty-eight states in the Union. The names of these states are carved into the exterior walls of the memorial.

Mount Rushmore

ount Rushmore is located in the Black Hills of South Dakota. The size and detail of this national monument are very impressive. In the early 1920s, an artist named Gutzon Borglum began to design sculptures for Mount Rushmore. He wanted to honor the United States's greatest leaders and celebrate the growth of the country. Construction of the monument began in 1927. Workers carved the faces of four U.S. presidents into the side of Mount Rushmore. The sculpture was completed in 1941. It cost nearly $1 million to create Mount Rushmore.

Gutzon Borglum died in 1941, leaving Roosevelt's sculpture incomplete. Borglum's son, Lincoln, finished the sculpture later that year.

The four American presidents carved into Mount Rushmore are George Washington, Thomas Jefferson, Abraham Lincoln, and Theodore Roosevelt. George Washington represents the country's fight for independence from Great Britain. Thomas Jefferson stands for a **democratic** government that is elected, or voted for, by the people. Abraham Lincoln represents the importance of equality and unity. Theodore Roosevelt stands for the United States's role in world affairs.

★ Gutzon Borglum's original design was a sculpture of the four presidents' heads and chests. However, there was only enough time and funds to sculpt the heads.

★ Each of the faces carved into Mount Rushmore is 60 feet high.

★ It took 400 workers to carve the faces on Mount Rushmore.

★ George Washington was the first sculpture completed. Thomas Jefferson was second, and Abraham Lincoln was third. The sculpture of Theodore Roosevelt's head was the last to be completed.

George Washington

More National Memorials

Special statues and monuments can be found across the United States. Some of the memorials honor important people in U.S. history. Others honor the U.S. soldiers who died serving the country during times of war.

★ Tomb of the Unknowns

The **Tomb** of the Unknowns is located in Arlington National Cemetery in Arlington, Virginia. The Tomb of the Unknowns was completed in 1931. It marks the graves of four unknown American soldiers from four different wars. The tomb is made of white marble and stands over 8 feet tall.

★ Korean War Veterans Memorial

The Korean War Veterans Memorial, completed in 1995, is located in Washington, D.C. It honors the soldiers who died during the Korean War (1950-1953). The memorial has nineteen statues of soldiers. The soldiers are from the four branches of the military: air force, army, Marine Corps, and navy. The memorial has a long granite, or rock, wall that displays more than 2,500 photographs of people who helped in the war effort.

★ Vietnam Veterans Memorial

The Vietnam Veterans Memorial is located in Washington, D.C. It honors the men and women who died during the Vietnam War. The memorial has three parts. One part is the Vietnam Veterans Memorial Wall, which lists the names of U.S. soldiers who died during the war.

★ Iwo Jima Memorial

The Iwo Jima Memorial is located in Arlington, Virginia. It honors all of the United States Marines who died in combat. The United States and Japan fought for control over the island of Iwo Jima in World War II. The memorial shows five marines and one navy soldier raising a U.S. flag on Iwo Jima. The statues of the soldiers stand 32 feet high. The flag they are raising flies from a 60-foot pole.

★ Thomas Jefferson Memorial

The Thomas Jefferson Memorial is located in Washington, D.C. This memorial honors Thomas Jefferson, the third U.S. president. Jefferson was also the author of the Declaration of Independence, and served as the first Secretary of State. The memorial is a circular, white marble monument. The inside walls of the monument are **inscribed** with his writings. At the center of the memorial is a 19-foot-tall bronze statue of Thomas Jefferson. It stands on a 6-foot-tall pedestal.

★ Franklin Delano Roosevelt Memorial

The Franklin Delano Roosevelt Memorial is located in Washington, D.C. It honors the thirty-second U.S. president. This memorial is one of the largest in the United States. It has sculptures, galleries, and waterfalls. The memorial also has four partially walled areas that contain bronze sculptures. The four rooms represent the four terms that Roosevelt served as president. Written on the walls of these rooms are some of Roosevelt's most famous quotes.

★ USS Arizona Memorial

The USS Arizona Memorial is a floating memorial. It is located in Pearl Harbor, off the coast of Honolulu, Hawai'i. The memorial was built to honor the more than 1,000 military workers who died on a battleship called *The USS Arizona*. The battleship was sunk on December 7, 1941, during an attack on Pearl Harbor. The memorial was completed in 1962. The names of those who died on *The USS Arizona* are engraved on the memorial's marble wall.

★ General Grant National Memorial

The General Grant National Memorial is located in New York City, New York. This monument is one of the largest tombs in North America. It is the tomb of General Ulysses S. Grant and his wife, Julia. General Grant was the eighteenth president of the United States. When he died in 1885, U.S. citizens wanted to honor him with a special monument. About 90,000 people donated money to build a structure to house his tomb. The General Grant National Memorial was completed in 1897.

★ Wright Brothers National Memorial

The Wright Brothers National Memorial is located near Kitty Hawk, North Carolina. This memorial honors the accomplishments of brothers Orville and Wilbur Wright. On December 17, 1903, the Wright brothers made the world's first successful flight. They flew over the Kill Devil Hills, in North Carolina. Today, a 60-foot monument stands in Kill Devil Hills. It is shaped like a pylon, or cone, and is made from granite.

★ Liberty Bell

The Liberty Bell represents freedom. It is located in Philadelphia, Pennsylvania. It weighs more than 2,000 pounds. In 1753, the bell was hung in Philadelphia's Independence Hall tower. For years, the bell rang out to mark special occasions. In the mid-1800s, the Liberty Bell cracked. Leaders worried that the crack would destroy the bell. They removed the bell from the tower. Today, the cracked Liberty Bell is on display at the Liberty Bell Pavilion.

★ Perry's Victory and International Peace Memorial

Perry's Victory and International Peace Memorial is located in Put-in-Bay, Ohio. This memorial honors Commodore Oliver Perry. During the War of 1812, Commodore Perry led a fleet, or group, of U.S. ships in a battle against British ships. Commodore Perry's troops won the battle, and the war ended soon after. This memorial marks Perry's victory and the peace that came after the battle. The memorial was completed in 1915. It stands 352 feet tall. It is the third tallest memorial in the country.

★ Benjamin Franklin National Memorial

The Benjamin Franklin National Memorial is located in Philadelphia, Pennsylvania. Benjamin Franklin helped write many important U.S. documents. He also started the first public library in the United States. The memorial is located in Memorial Hall at The Franklin Institute Science Museum. It has a 20-foot-high marble statue of Franklin. The statue sits on a pedestal and weighs 30 tons.

Memorials Everywhere

There are special memorials across the United States. This map shows the locations of the national memorials mentioned in this book. Are any of these memorials located in your state?

1. **Franklin Delano Roosevelt Memorial**: Washington, D.C.

2. **Iwo Jima Memorial**: Washington, D.C.

3. **Korean War Veterans Memorial**: Washington, D.C.

4. **Lincoln Memorial**: Washington, D.C.

5. **Thomas Jefferson Memorial**: Washington, D.C.

6. **Vietnam Veterans Memorial**: Washington, D.C.

7. **Washington Monument**: Washington, D.C.

8. **Benjamin Franklin National Memorial**: Philadelphia, Pennsylvania

9. **General Grant National Memorial**: New York City, New York

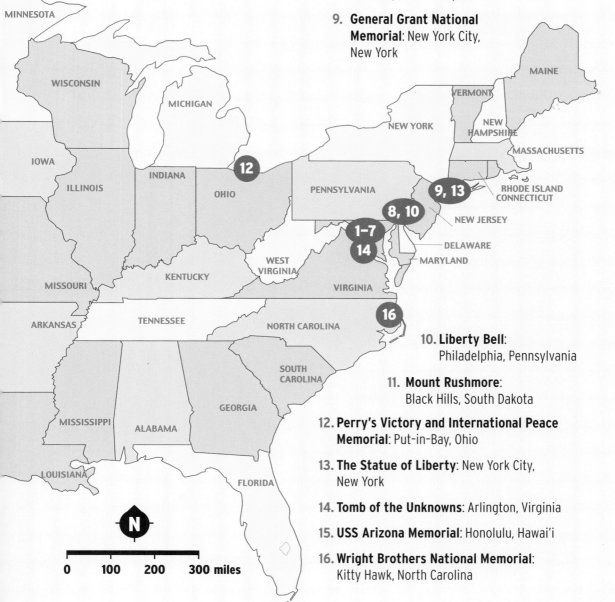

10. **Liberty Bell**: Philadelphia, Pennsylvania

11. **Mount Rushmore**: Black Hills, South Dakota

12. **Perry's Victory and International Peace Memorial**: Put-in-Bay, Ohio

13. **The Statue of Liberty**: New York City, New York

14. **Tomb of the Unknowns**: Arlington, Virginia

15. **USS Arizona Memorial**: Honolulu, Hawai'i

16. **Wright Brothers National Memorial**: Kitty Hawk, North Carolina

America's Statues

Some of the most impressive statues in the country are found in the U.S. Capitol's National Statuary Hall Collection. Every state has donated statues to this collection. The statues represent important people in each state's history.

STATE	DONATED STATUES
Alabama	Jabez Lamar Monroe Curry and Joseph Wheeler
Alaska	Edward Lewis Bartlett and Ernest Gruening
Arizona	John Campbell Greenway and Eusebio F. Kino
Arkansas	James Paul Clarke and Uriah Milton Rose
California	Thomas Starr King and Father Junipero Serra
Colorado	Florence R. Sabin and John L. Swigert
Connecticut	Roger Sherman and Jonathan Trumbull
Delaware	John Middleton Clayton and Caesar Rodney
Florida	John Gorrie and Edmund Kirby Smith
Georgia	Crawford W. Long and Alexander Hamilton Stephens
Hawai'i	Father Damien and Kamehameha I
Idaho	William Edgar Borah and George Laird Shoup
Illinois	James Shields and Frances E. Willard
Indiana	Oliver Hazard Perry Morton and Lewis Wallace
Iowa	James Harlan and Samuel Jordan Kirkwood
Kansas	John James Ingalls and George Washington Glick
Kentucky	Henry Clay and Ephraim McDowell
Louisiana	Huey Pierce Long and Edward Douglass White
Maine	Hannibal Hamlin and William King
Maryland	Charles Carroll and John Hanson
Massachusetts	Samuel Adams and John Winthrop
Michigan	Lewis Cass and Zachariah Chandler

Minnesota	Henry Mower Rice and Maria L. Sanford
Mississippi	Jefferson Davis and James Zachariah George
Missouri	Thomas Hart Benton and Francis Preston Blair, Jr.
Montana	Jeannette Rankin and Charles Marion Russell
Nebraska	William Jennings Bryan and Julius Sterling Morton
Nevada	Patrick Anthony McCarran
New Hampshire	John Stark and Daniel Webster
New Jersey	Philip Kearny and Richard Stockton
New Mexico	Dennis Chavez
New York	George Clinton and Robert R. Livingston
North Carolina	Charles Brantley Aycock and Zebulon Baird Vance
North Dakota	John Burke
Ohio	William Allen and James A. Garfield
Oklahoma	Will Rogers and Sequoyah
Oregon	Jason Lee and John McLoughlin
Pennsylvania	Robert Fulton and John Peter Gabriel Muhlenberg
Rhode Island	Nathanael Greene and Roger Williams
South Carolina	John Caldwell Calhoun and Wade Hampton
South Dakota	William Henry Harrison Beadle and Joseph Ward
Tennessee	Andrew Jackson and John Sevier
Texas	Stephen Austin and Sam Houston
Utah	Philo T. Farnsworth and Brigham Young
Vermont	Ethan Allen and Jacob Collamer
Virginia	Robert E. Lee and George Washington
Washington	Mother Joseph and Marcus Whitman
West Virginia	John E. Kenna and Francis Harrison Pierpont
Wisconsin	Robert M. La Follette and Jacques Marquette
Wyoming	Esther Hobart Morris and Washakie

Further Research

Many statues and monuments in the United States have fascinating histories. Some have become symbols of the United States's heritage, or traditions. These Web sites and books can help you learn more.

Independence Day fireworks explode in the sky around the Statue of Liberty.

Web Sites

★ To learn more about monuments in the United States, visit:
www.americanhistory.about.com/cs/monuments

★ To learn more about the National Statuary Hall Collection, visit:
www.aoc.gov/cc/art/nsh/nsh_states.htm

★ Discover how Mount Rushmore was created at:
www.travelsd.com/parks/rushmore

Books

★ Drummond, Allan. *Liberty!* New York: Frances Foster Books, 2002

★ Ashabranner, Brent K. *On the Mall in Washington, D.C.: A Visit to America's Front Yard.* Breckenridge: Twenty First Century Books, 2001

Create Your Own Monument

American citizens build memorials to honor important people and events. Imagine that you were asked to create a monument or statue that honors an important person or event in your life. Who or what would you choose to honor? What sort of memorial would you build? Would it be a statue like the Statue of Liberty? Would you create a memorial like the Washington Monument? Draw a picture of the memorial you would create. Below the picture, explain what the symbols in your memorial mean.

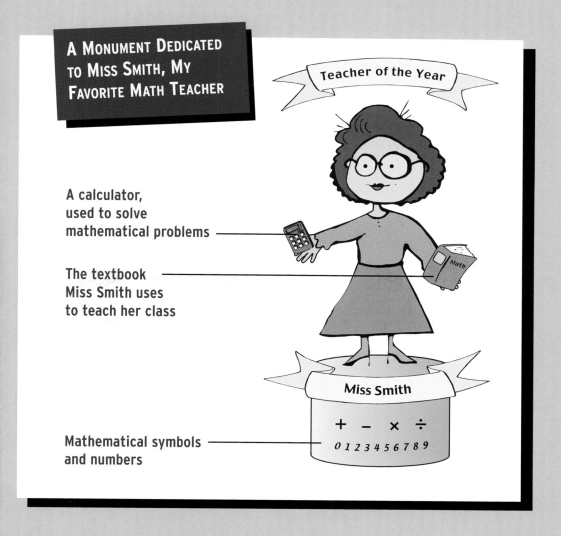

A MONUMENT DEDICATED TO MISS SMITH, MY FAVORITE MATH TEACHER

Teacher of the Year

A calculator, used to solve mathematical problems

The textbook Miss Smith uses to teach her class

Miss Smith

Mathematical symbols and numbers

+ − × ÷

0 1 2 3 4 5 6 7 8 9

Glossary

★ **American Revolution:** a war fought between the U.S. and Great Britain from 1775 to 1783

★ **assassinated:** killed

★ **Civil War:** the war fought in the United States between the North and the South from 1861 to 1865

★ **cornerstone:** a stone that has writing on it that is placed in the corner of a building

★ **democratic:** a system of government in which all people are believed to be equal

★ **immigrants:** people who move to another country

★ **independence:** not ruled by another country

★ **inscribed:** written, marked

★ **justice:** fair decisions or treatment

★ **obelisk:** a tall, stone column with four decorated sides and a pointed top

★ **pedestal:** a column that supports a statue or monument

★ **tablet:** a flat surface of metal, stone, or wood that has writing on it

★ **temple:** a place of worship

★ **tomb:** a stone building or underground room where someone is buried

★ **tyranny:** unfair ruling or treatment

★ **Union:** all of the American states that united as one nation

Index